MALI

MALI

CROSSROADS OF AFRICA

PHILIP KOSLOW

CHELSEA HOUSE PUBLISHERS • New York • Philadelphia

Frontispiece: A terra-cotta statue created between 1300 and 1400 in the city of Jenne in Mali.

On the Cover: An artist's rendering of a terra-cotta sculpture from ancient Mali; in the background, a traditional Mandingo village in the Niger River region.

CHELSEA HOUSE PUBLISHERS

Editorial Director   Richard Rennert
Executive Managing Editor   Karyn Gullen Browne
Copy Chief   Robin James
Picture Editor   Adrian G. Allen
Art Director   Robert Mitchell
Manufacturing Director   Gerald Levine
Assistant Art Director   Joan Ferrigno

THE KINGDOMS OF AFRICA
Senior Editor   Martin Schwabacher

Staff for MALI
Assistant Editor   Catherine Iannone
Editorial Assistant   Sydra Mallery
Designer   Cambraia Magalhães
Picture Researcher   Wendy Wills
Cover Illustrator   Bradford Brown

First Printing
1 3 5 7 9 8 6 4 2

Library of Congress Cataloging-in-Publication Data

Koslow, Philip.
  Mali: The Land of Gold/Philip Koslow
    p. cm.—(Kingdoms of Africa)
Includes bibliographical references and index.
  ISBN   0-7910-3127-6
         0-7910-2942-5 (pbk.)
    1. Mali—History—Juvenile literature. [1. Mali—History.] I. Title. II. Series.
DT551.65.K67 1995
966.23—dc20

94-26193
CIP
AC

CONTENTS

Titles in
THE KINGDOMS OF AFRICA

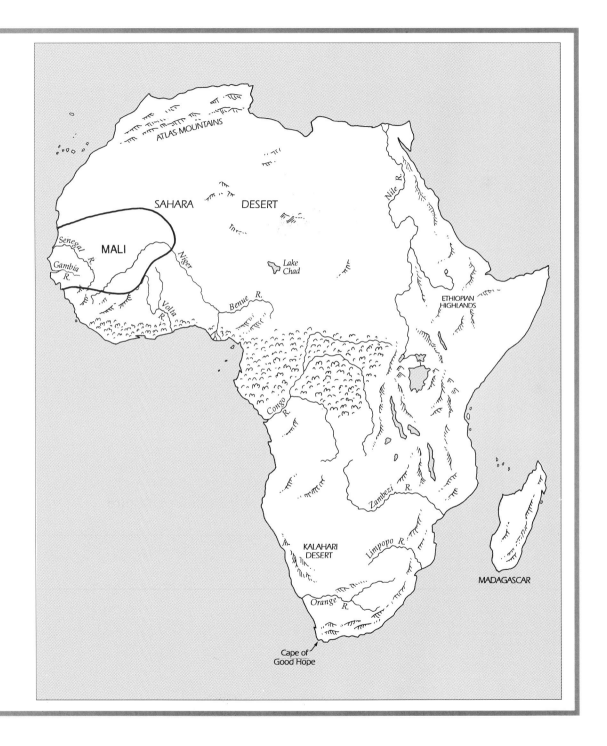

"CIVILIZATION AND MAGNIFICENCE"

A relief map of Africa indicating the territory controlled by the empire of Mali.

O n a sunny morning in July 1796, Mungo Park, a Scottish doctor turned explorer, achieved a major goal of his long and difficult trek through West Africa when he reached the banks of the mighty Niger River. Along the river was a cluster of four large towns, which together made up the city of Segu, the principal settlement of the Bambara people. The sight of Segu dazzled Park as much as the spectacle of the broad, shining waterway. "The view of this extensive city," he wrote, "the numerous canoes upon the river; the crowded population; and the cultivated state of the surrounding country, found altogether a prospect of civilization and magnificence, which I little expected to find in the bosom of Africa."

Park's account of his journey, *Travels in the Interior Districts of Africa*, became a best-seller in England. But his positive reflections on Africa were soon brushed aside by the English and other Europeans, who were engaged in a profitable trade in slaves along the West African coast and would eventually carve up the entire continent into colonies. Later explorers such as Richard Burton, who spoke of the "childishness" and "backwardness" of Africans, achieved more lasting fame than did Park, who drowned during a second expedition to Africa in 1806. Thus it is not surprising that 100 years after Park's arrival at Segu, a professor at Oxford University in England wrote with bland self-assurance that African history before the arrival of Europeans had been nothing more than "blank, uninteresting, brutal barbarism." The professor's opinion was published when the British Empire was at its height, and it represented a point of view that was necessary to justify the exploitation of Africans. If, as the professor

7

Mungo Park (1771–1806) was among the first Europeans to report accurately on West Africa. About the region's inhabitants he wrote, "Of all the countries in the world their own appears to them as the best, and their own people as the happiest."

claimed, Africans had lived in a state of chaos throughout their history, then their European conquerors could believe that they were doing a noble deed by imposing their will and their way of life upon Africa.

The colonialist view of African history held sway into the 20th century. But as the century progressed, more enlightened scholars began to take a fresh look at Africa's past. As archaeologists (scientists who study the physical remains of past societies) explored the sites of former African cities, they found that Africans had enjoyed a high level of civilization hundreds of years before the arrival of Europeans. In many respects the kingdoms and cities of Africa had been equal to or more advanced than European societies during the same period.

Modern scientists also reject the idea—fostered by Europeans during the time of the slave trade and colonialism—that there is any connection between a people's skin color and their capacity for achievement and self-government. Differences in pigmentation, scientists now recognize, are based solely upon climate and have nothing to do with intellectual ability. When the human species began to develop in the torrid regions of Africa some 7.5 million years ago, humans were all dark skinned because dark pigmentation protected them from the harmful ultraviolet rays of the sun. However, when humans later migrated from Africa to colder climates where there was far less sunlight, heavy pigmentation became a drawback—it prevented the skin from absorbing the amount of sunlight needed to produce vitamin D, which is essential for the growth of bones and teeth. Hence lighter skin began to predominate in Europe, with the peoples of Asia, the Middle East, and North Africa occupying a middle ground between Europeans and dark-skinned Africans. Rather than indicating superiority, therefore, lighter skin can be viewed as a divergence from the original pigmentation of all human beings.

As early as 400 B.C., a West African people centered in the village of Nok, in present-day Nigeria, produced small sculptures equal in workmanship and beauty to anything created by the widely acclaimed artists of ancient Greece and Rome. By A.D. 750, when most of Europe was still mired in the Dark Ages, the prosperous kingdom

of ancient Ghana, known as the Land of Gold, flourished in West Africa. Control of the gold trade kept Ghana powerful through the 12th century, but invasions from ambitious neighbors and the gradual exhaustion of the kingdom's goldfields gradually took their toll. By the 13th century, an even greater empire than Ghana's emerged to dominate the West African landscape and forge greater links between Africa and the rest of the world.

Chapter 1 | THE LION OF MALI

The West African kingdom of ancient Ghana, founded by the Soninke people, depended for its wealth on the goldfields of Bambuk, located between the Senegal and Faleme rivers. After more than four centuries of mining operations, the gold of Bambuk showed signs of running out. A new source of the precious metal was discovered at Bure along the Niger River, well to the southeast of Ghana's territory. Weakened by attacks from their northern neighbors, the once-powerful Ghanaians were incapable of extending their rule to Bure.

The goldfields of Bure lay in the territory of the Malinke, a division of the Mandingo people, who were renowned as warriors and traders. Like the Soninke, the Malinke spoke a language that belonged to the Mande family, the domi-

A view of the village of Kirina, the site of the epic battle between Sundiata and Sumanguru in 1240. Sundiata's dramatic victory on the plains of Kirina gave birth to the empire of Mali.

nant language group of West Africa. However, the Malinke had not followed the pattern of the Soninke in developing a unified state headed by a single king. Instead, they had continued to live in communities known as *kafu*s. A kafu was a collection of villages whose total population might range from 10,000 to as much as 50,000. Each kafu was ruled by a *mansa*, or chief, who was usually the head of a major descent line that traced its origin to a powerful ancestor.

Ghana had become a centralized state in order to deal successfully with traders from North Africa, who were eager to trade much-needed salt from the Sahara Desert for the gold of the Sudan. (In the Arabic language, spoken by the North Africans, West Africa was called *Bilad al-Sudan,* "the land of the black peoples.")

11

Because the Malinke did not respond quickly to the opportunity presented by the riches of Bure, it was inevitable that another group would seize the initiative.

In 1203, Sumanguru Kante, king of the neighboring Soso people, captured the Ghanaian capital of Kumbi Saleh and sought to make himself master of the gold trade. At the same time, his powerful army subjugated the Malinke and gained control of Bure. However, the North African traders who lived in Kumbi Saleh found Sumanguru greedy and overbearing, and they refused to pay his excessive taxes. The traders abandoned their settlement at Kumbi Saleh and traveled north to the edge of the Sahara, where they set up a new trading center at Walata. From there, they could still conduct trade with the gold producers of Bambuk and avoid bringing their goods through Sumanguru's territory.

The traders clearly hoped that Sumanguru's reign would be short-lived. The Malinke whom he had conquered were not a people to remain long in subjection. Before long, a serious challenge to Sumanguru arose from the Malinke state of Kangaba, under the leadership of Sundiata Keita.

In the villages of present-day West Africa, including Kangaba, storytellers known as *griots* still sing the praises of Sundiata, who is also known by the titles Mari Diata (Lord Lion), the Lion of Mali, and Father of the Bright Country. During the colonial period, Europeans generally scorned the accounts of these bards, deeming them of little historical value. Recent scholars, however, have recognized that the *oral traditions* of the African peoples are just as valuable as the written records of Arab or European societies. During the 1960s, for example, the Senegalese scholar Djibril Niane recorded the words of Djeli Mamoudou Kouyate, a griot living in the village of Djeliba Koro, in the nation of Guinea. "We are the vessels of speech," the griot proudly declared at the opening of his saga. "We are the repositories which harbor secrets many centuries old; without us the names of kings would vanish into oblivion, we are the memory of mankind; by the spoken word we bring to life the deeds and exploits of kings for younger generations."

According to Kouyate's narrative, Sundiata was the son of a great Mandingo king, Maghan Kon Fatta, and the king's second wife, Sogolon Kedjou. (West African kings normally had a principal wife and one or more additional wives.) The child's birth was hailed as a great event, but Sundiata's early years were most unpromising. Though gifted with great strength and a thoughtful nature, he could not bend his legs. For the first seven years of his life he had to crawl about, to the despair of his mother and the delight of the king's principal wife, Sassouma Berete. When the king died, Sassouma saw to it that her own son, Dankaran Tuma, ascended the throne, despite Maghan Kon Fatta's stated wish that Sundiata succeed him. "People had seen one-eyed kings, one-armed kings, and lame kings," the griot related, "but a stiff-legged king had never been heard tell of." Still jealous of Sogolon and her son, Sassouma had them banished to a hut behind the palace.

Shortly thereafter, Sundiata's disability was cured with the aid of Farakourou, the royal blacksmith. (Because the working of iron into tools and weapons was so crucial to the development of African kingdoms, Africans often regarded the blacksmith as an individual possessed of magical powers.) By the age of 10, Sundiata was a skilled hunter and a natural leader. The ill will of Sassouma now increased, and Sogolon decided that she and her children would be safer away from Niani, the royal city. With the aid of traveling merchants, they journeyed

This statuette from ancient Mali is believed to represent Sogolon, the mother of Sundiata. According to Mandingo traditions, Sogolon was unusually ugly; nevertheless, the king of Mali chose her as a wife after a soothsayer predicted that Sogolon would give birth to Mali's greatest hero.

westward to Kumbi Saleh, the capital of ancient Ghana, and after a brief stay went on to Mema on the Niger.

When he was 15, Sundiata took part in his first military campaign. His

A clay sculpture of an archer from ancient Mali. Mande-speaking peoples such as the Malinke, who founded the empire of Mali, achieved military dominance in large part because of their skill in fashioning iron arrowheads, lances, and swords.

14

strength and bravery in battle, as well as his mental capacity, soon made him the favorite of Mansa Tunkara, the king of Mema. At the age of 18, Sundiata became the king's most trusted adviser. "At that time," the griot related, "he was a tall young man with a fat neck and a powerful chest. Nobody else could bend his bow. Everyone bowed before him and he was greatly loved."

In contrast to Sundiata, Dankaran Tuma had proved to be a feeble character, dominated by his mother. When Sumanguru moved to crush the Mandingo revolt, Dankaran Tuma fled the kingdom. Having learned of Sundiata's feats in exile, Mandingo messengers journeyed to Mema and begged him to return. Sundiata agreed, and accompanied by a group of soldiers from Mema, he set out for home.

After gathering the Mandingo forces, Sundiata took up a position along the Niger and announced his determination to drive Sumanguru from Mali. (In the Mande language, *Mali* means "where the king resides.") Sundiata's cause was greatly aided by Sumanguru's nephew Fakoli, who came over to the Mandingo after Sumanguru stole his wife. Fakoli had been one of Sumanguru's best commanders, and the addition of Fakoli's loyal troops was a great benefit to the Mandingo. In 1240, the two armies met on the plain of Kirina. Djeli Mamoudou Kouyate gives the following account of the battle:

> [Sundiata] and his cavalry charged with great dash but they were stopped by the horsemen of Diaghan and a struggle to the death began. Tabon Wana and the archers of Wagadou stretched out their lines toward the hills and the battle spread over the entire plain, while an unrelenting sun climbed in the sky. The horses of Mema were extremely agile, and they reared forward with their fore hooves raised and swooped down on the horsemen of Diaghan, who rolled on the ground trampled under the horses' hooves. Presently the men of Diaghan gave ground and fell back towards the rear. The enemy center was broken.

At this point, Sundiata went in search of Sumanguru, who had led an attack on the forces of Fakoli. Sumanguru had no wish to fight Sundiata and hid from him in the thick of the battle. At last, Sundiata saw his enemy in the distance and let fly an arrow from his powerful bow. The arrow merely grazed Sumanguru's shoulder, but that was enough. Sundiata had already learned that Sumanguru's magic protected him only against wounds inflicted by iron weapons; therefore, his arrow was tipped with the spur of a rooster, and when it tore Sumanguru's flesh, the king's power deserted him. "Now trembling like a man in the grip of fever, the vanquished [Sumanguru] looked up toward the sun. A great black bird flew over above the fray and he understood. It was a bird of misfortune."

Sumanguru fled and disappeared into the mountains, never to be seen again. The victorious Sundiata destroyed the once-powerful city of Soso—"now a spot where guinea fowl and young partridges come to take their dust baths," according to the griot. Sundiata created a constitution for the Mandingo and set about subduing all the kings of the immediate area. By the time of his death in 1270, he had transformed his kingdom into an empire and had truly earned the title Lion of Mali.

15

Chapter 2 | THE GROWTH OF EMPIRE

Muslims partake in the traditional Friday prayer outside an ancient mosque in San, Mali. The rulers of Mali adopted Islam during the 13th century, realizing that the new religion would create a powerful bond between North African traders and the peoples of the Sudan.

As the empire of Mali grew, it began to surpass by a wide margin the amount of territory formerly controlled by the kings of ancient Ghana. The two kingdoms differed in other significant ways, including their attitudes toward the outside world. The North African traders who came to Ghana's capital city, Kumbi Saleh, were valued for the wealth they brought and were given special consideration. They did not have to kneel and cover their heads with dust in the presence of the king as did ordinary subjects; instead, they were allowed to greet the monarch simply by clapping their hands. However, the kings of Ghana took great pains to keep themselves aloof from the customs and religion of the North African traders. Because centralized rule was a new experience to the peoples of West Africa, the kings were especially eager to maintain the loyalty of their people by upholding the ancient religious faith of the Soninke.

By the time of Sundiata, however, kingship was an established tradition in West Africa, and the peoples of the Sudan had been exposed for 500 years or more to influences from the east and the north. It was inevitable that the rulers, at least, would eventually feel the influence of one of the most powerful forces at work in the world of the 13th century—the religion of Islam.

Islam had arisen in the deserts of Arabia, to the east of Africa. The inhabitants of Arabia, who were mainly farmers and wandering herders, had for centuries worshiped a variety of gods and spirits, many of them associated with forces of nature. In this form of worship, the Arabians were following the earliest inhabitants of the Middle East, peoples such as the Sumerians and Assyrians, who had created the world's first great civilizations. As they honored these age-old beliefs, however, the Arabians were in close contact with peoples who practiced more recent religions, such as Judaism and Christianity. Both Judaism and Christianity were based upon worship of a single god. Both religions had been founded by powerful figures who had experienced what they believed to be a direct communication from God, revealing a great truth for all humanity.

The prophet who emerged to express a new religious idea in Arabia was named Muhammad. Born in the city of Mecca in 570, Muhammad spent his youth as a camel driver and then became a tradesman. At the age of 40, he had a vision of a new religion based on the worship of a single god, Allah, who demanded strict devotion, regular prayer, and pure habits in return for eternal salvation. Muhammad quickly attracted a group of followers, but he also aroused bitter opposition among the Arabian tribespeople, who felt that he was attacking their traditional beliefs and way of life. In 622, Muhammad's enemies forced him to leave Mecca and resettle in Medina. There he continued to gather converts, who became known as Muslims, and to develop the principles that grew into the religion of Islam. By the time of Muhammad's death in 632, his influence had spread throughout Arabia. His teachings were recorded in the holy book known as the Koran, which has the same importance for Muslims that the Old Testament has for Jews and the New Testament has for Christians.

Muhammad's followers, led by the prophet's father-in-law, Abu Bakr, set out to spread their faith and culture. By 645, Muslim warriors had conquered all of Arabia and much of the Middle East. From there they moved westward into the central part of North Africa, known as the Maghrib. By the end of the 7th century, the Muslims had extended their power to the Atlantic coast of Africa, and shortly afterward they crossed the Strait of Gibraltar to conquer much of present-day Spain and Portugal.

The Muslims of North Africa did not attempt to extend their rule to West Africa; the undertaking would have been too difficult, and they had more to gain from maintaining friendly relations with their trading partners. Even though Muslims were convinced that they had received the word of God, they were known for their general tolerance in religious matters. They made no attempt to convert Christians and Jews, whom they considered "peoples of the Book," and they converted peoples they considered "pagans" only when there was a political advantage in doing so. As long as the kings of Ghana allowed the Muslims to build their mosques in the Sudan's trading centers and gather for prayer at the appointed hours, there was no reason to impose Islam on West Africans.

In the course of time, some Muslim groups adopted a more aggressive stance. The Sanhaja, a warlike tribe of the southern Sahara, began raiding the Sudanese kingdom of Takrur during the 10th and 11th centuries. In order to appease the Sanhaja, the rulers of Takrur converted to Islam. Takrur later became an ally of an even more powerful and militant Muslim group known as the Almoravids. After the Almoravids captured Kumbi Saleh, Ghana's capital city, in 1037, they converted many of the local people to Islam. After this, the way was open for far greater Muslim influence in the Sudan.

According to the Israeli historian Nehemiah Levtzion, who has carefully examined Arabic writings of the period, Islam came to Mali gradually, as a result of contacts between Muslim holy men

19

Muhammad ascending to Heaven, as depicted in a Persian miniature. The religion of Islam, founded by Muhammad during the 7th century, rapidly spread throughout the Middle East and North Africa, powerfully affecting the spiritual and cultural life of both regions.

20

and the Malinke chiefs who played host to trading caravans. The Arab writer al-Bakri, for example, described at length how the chief of a community suffering from drought was persuaded by a Muslim teacher that Allah could solve his problem:

> He persisted with the king until the latter sincerely adopted Islam. . . . Then the Muslim asked the king to wait until the night of the following Friday, when he told him to be purified by a complete ablution [ritual washing], and clothed him in a cotton robe he had with him. . . . They prayed throughout the night; the Muslim reciting invocations, and the king saying the amen. The dawn had just begun to break, when Allah brought down abundant rain. . . . Then the king ordered that the idols be broken and the sorcerers expelled from the country.

Aspiring empire builders such as Sundiata understood the advantages of Islam. As a universal religion, one that recognized (at least in theory) the equality of all believers regardless of tribe, race, or nationality, Islam could be a powerful binding force between the diverse peoples of a large empire. In addition, the intellectual aspects of Islamic society—especially the arts of reading and writing—could be ex-

This 14th-century kneeling figure from the Niger region of Mali may have been connected with traditional ancestor worship. Though the religion of Islam had a marked influence in the cities of West Africa, the people of the countryside continued to follow their age-old beliefs.

tremely useful in the organization of government.

In contrast to Islam, the religions practiced by most West Africans were similar to the pre-Islamic beliefs of the desert tribes in Arabia. However much wealth their rulers accumulated through the gold trade, West Africans still depended on agriculture for their survival. Like all farmers, they had learned to regard the forces of nature with awe. This was all the more reasonable in Africa, a continent that had challenged its human inhabitants for millions of years with droughts, torrential rains, fierce heat, ferocious wild animals, and deadly diseases. West African religions, therefore, were based on the idea of harmony between the people and the land—for this reason, many of their sacred figures were animals, such as the snake and the ram. Many African religions did include a supreme being or creator-god whose power set in motion many other forces. But the idea of a single all-powerful god with no earthly form, not to mention a holy book written in a strange language, did not hold great appeal for the hardwork-

ing farmers and fishers who made up the mass of the West African population.

Because of this split between the culture of the cities and the culture of the countryside, Sundiata and the other Malinke chiefs had to walk a fine line. For all the advantage they might gain by converting to Islam, they could not forget that the base of their power rested on the people who provided food for the cities and filled the ranks of the army in time of war. Any suggestion that the ruler was no longer the guardian of age-old beliefs and traditions would remove a major prop from his authority. The Muslims themselves apparently understood this dilemma; they rarely expected their royal converts to be devout Muslims, asking only that they learn a few rituals and a few passages from the Koran. As the historian Basil Davidson has pointed out, Sundiata always presented himself to his own people as a guardian of Malinke tradition and as "a powerful man of magic and enchantment." When some of his successors forgot this lesson, they paid a high price for their mistake.

21

Chapter 3 | MANSA MUSA

A section of the Catalan Atlas of Charles V *(completed in 1375) contains the only known image of Mansa Musa. The mapmaker, Abraham Cresques, depicted the great king of Mali seated on his throne, holding a large nugget of gold.*

According to the oral traditions of the Malinke, Sundiata ruled Mali for 25 years and was followed by his son Mansa Uli. Under Mansa Uli's regime, the borders of Mali began to expand in all directions, and eventually they encompassed an area at least twice as large as that formerly controlled by the kings of Ghana. At its height, Mali included not only Ghana's former possessions but also extended to the Niger River, bringing the important trading cities of Gao, Jenne, and Timbuktu—as well as both the Bambuk and Bure goldfields—under the control of Mali's rulers.

Perhaps the most illustrious of Mali's rulers was Mansa Musa, who ruled from 1312 to 1337. Though two of his predecessors, Mansa Uli and Sakura, had conquered vast territories, it was Mansa Musa who finally brought Mali to the attention of the world. His pilgrimage to Mecca, the holy city of Islam, in 1324 was an event of such importance that Arab historians were still speaking of it centuries later.

Mansa Musa's journey from Niani to Mecca took an entire year. His caravan reportedly included 100 camels, each laden with 300 pounds of gold. The king was accompanied by thousands of his subjects, who included slaves, soldiers, and dignitaries. The king's senior wife, Inare Kunate, was herself attended by 500 maids and slaves. According to one account, undoubtedly somewhat exaggerated, the caravan was so long that the head of it reached Timbuktu while Mansa

24

Musa was still more than 200 miles away in his palace at Niani, preparing for his departure.

The 15th-century Arab writer al-Makrizi described Mansa Musa's arrival in Cairo: "He was a young man with a brown skin, a pleasant face and a good figure, instructed in the Malikite [orthodox Muslim] rite. He appeared amongst his companions magnificently dressed and mounted, and surrounded by more than ten thousand of his subjects. He brought gifts and presents that amazed the eye with their beauty and splendor."

Although Mansa Musa was obliged to kneel before the sultan of Egypt, who was perhaps the most powerful figure in the Muslim world, he was generally treated by the Egyptians as an important personage. The sultan gave his distinguished visitor the use of a palace during his stay, fitted him and his closest advisers with luxurious robes, and promised Mansa Musa full provisions for his journey from Cairo to Mecca.

According to Nehemiah Levtzion, Mansa Musa lavishly rewarded the hospitality of his hosts, doing his best to show them that his kingdom was no less wealthy than theirs: "He gave presents of gold to the Egyptian sultan and to those Egyptian officials who looked after him.

Among the possessions of the . . . official responsible for the reception of important visitors, there were thousands of ingots of raw gold presented to him by the Sudanese ruler. So much gold was brought to Cairo by Mansa Musa, distributed there as presents and spent in the markets, that the value of gold decreased considerably, from ten to twenty five percent, according to the different sources." Levtzion also points out that the merchants of the Egyptian capital regarded the Sudanese visitors as fair game, overcharging them by as much as five times for the items they purchased. Mansa Musa himself fell victim to the Egyptian moneylenders on his return journey. Having given away or spent all his gold, he was forced to borrow money for his trip back to Niani at steep rates of interest: for every 300 dinars he borrowed, he had to pay back 700.

Apparently, the vast expenditures of the trip did nothing to diminish Mansa Musa's wealth or power. Indeed, the pilgrimage to Mecca appears to have been a great success from every point of view. In Egypt and Arabia, he had been able to forge alliances and trade agreements with rulers and merchants. While passing through his territories, he was able to assure the loyalty of his subjects with

(Continued on page 29)

SCULPTURE OF JENNE

In the 1940s, exquisite terra-cotta statues were discovered in the area of Jenne. Archaeologists believe that they date from the 11th to the 14th centuries, but little is known about their function or significance. It has been suggested that some of these figures represent ancestors and were placed in family shrines.

The figure of a seated prisoner, dating from the 13th or 14th century.

Fragment of a figure with serpents on the stomach and head, c. 13th century.

Crouching figure with hands covering the face, c. 1400.

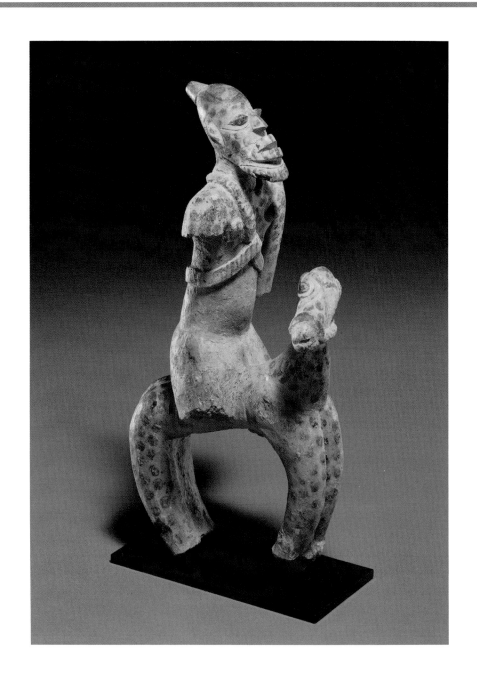

Equestrian figure.

(Continued from page 24)

gifts and honors and to reassert control over those localities, such as the city of Gao, that were showing signs of independence. To the inhabitants of Mali's empire, the sudden advent of the great king, accompanied by a massive caravan and a host of officials, soldiers, and servants, must have been a daunting and awe-inspiring spectacle.

In his emotional reaction to the pilgrimage, Mansa Musa revealed the depth of his religious feeling. Apparently, the experience of visiting Mecca and standing before the tomb of Muhammad made a deep impression on the king. According to the Arab writer al-Umari, "he returned to his country with the intention of abdicating in favor of his son and leaving all power in his hands, so that he might return to Venerable Mecca to live in the neighborhood of its sanctuary." By the time he was back in Niani, however, Mansa Musa's political instincts had taken over once again. There is evidence in the Malinke traditions that the returning king presented himself to his people as being more than ever the champion of the ancestral religions. In the eyes of the Sudanese, Mansa Musa's pilgrimage to Mecca, rather than signaling a change of faith, only increased the aura of his religious power.

A representation of Mecca from a 19th-century Syrian manuscript. The birthplace of Muhammad, Mecca is the holy city of Islam. Islamic law requires that all Muslims make a pilgrimage to Mecca at least once in a lifetime if they have the means to do so.

29

Nevertheless, the pilgrimage had long-lasting effects on the people of Mali. Mansa Musa had been impressed by

30

This 1861 painting by the French artist Léon Belly depicts a group of pilgrims on their way to Mecca. During the Middle Ages, some 50,000 worshipers made the pilgrimage each year; few traveled in such splendor as Mansa Musa, whose retinue included thousands of his subjects.

many facets of Muslim culture, and he was determined to bring these influences to bear in his own country. On his return journey he was accompanied by Abu Ishaq as-Sahili, a poet and architect from Muslim Spain. He had also recruited from Mecca four descendants of Muhammad, known as *sharufa,* who agreed to accompany him to Mali in return for 1,000 dinars apiece. Because the sharufa enjoyed a special status in the Muslim world, their presence in Niani would add a great deal of prestige to Mansa Musa's court and make Mali even more appealing to Muslim traders.

As a result of his pilgrimage, the name of Mansa Musa became known not only in Egypt and Arabia but throughout Europe. At this time European rulers were beginning to mint gold coins; they were eager to acquire Sudanese gold, which was considered to be the best available. Thus the faraway land of Mali, which no European had ever seen, exerted a powerful allure on them. For example, an important map of Africa drawn up by the 14th-century mapmaker Abraham Cresques, a Portuguese Jew, features the figure of Mansa Musa at the center of African trade routes. In the map, the king, dressed in a crown and royal robes, is seated on his throne, holding out a huge nugget of gold to a trader mounted on a camel. The legend on the map describes Mansa Musa as "the richest and most noble king in all the land."

31

Chapter 4 | THE CROSSROADS OF AFRICA

The house of a Muslim official in Jenne, photographed during the 19th century. During the great days of the Malian empire, river ports such as Jenne, Timbuktu, Gao, and Mopti impressed visitors with their size and prosperity.

When Mansa Musa returned from Mecca with the architect as-Sahili, the face of Mali began to change. As-Sahili built a new mosque in Timbuktu and a palace for Mansa Musa in Niani. Previously, even the kings' palaces in the Sudan had followed the traditional plan, being circular in design with conical roofs. Muslims, on the other hand, favored rectangular houses with flat roofs. In cities such as Kumbi Saleh it had always been easy to distinguish, by the style of building, the settlement of the Muslim traders from the quarters occupied by the Sudanese. But in Mali the distinction began to blur. In his book *African Cities and Towns Before the European Conquest*, Richard W. Hull has described the influence of Islam on the Sudanese way of building:

> Malekite law insisted on a square or rectangular Friday mosque; and Sudanic monarchs made every effort to construct their palaces in the idiom of the mosque. It became prestigious to live and worship in structures mirroring those of the Holy Land. Thus, from the fourteenth century, centers such as Timbuktu, Djenné, and Gao took on the appearance of Middle Eastern or North African cities. However, the architectural style was unique in that, without stone or long timbers, buildings had to be constructed with mud bricks and short wooden branches gathered from local scrubland. These materials dictated a pyramidal verticality and an extensive

wooden superstructure. The exterior walls exhibited a prickly effect as the small wooden sticks protruded from the wood surface.

The Muslim holy men and teachers who returned to Mali with Mansa Musa also established schools and law courts. The Muslim schools, famed throughout the world, had a major impact on West Africa. Because the religion of Islam centered upon the study and observance of the Koran, reading and writing were all-

34

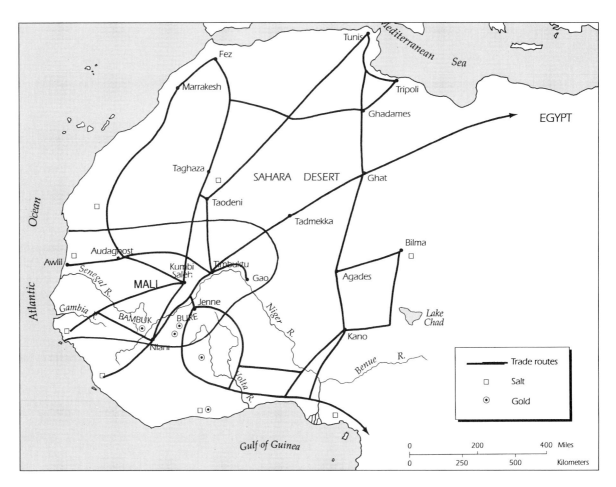

A map of the western Sudan, showing major trade routes and the boundaries of the empire of Mali. During the 14th and 15th centuries, Mali was the world's major source of high-quality gold; by collecting duties from the gold trade and other forms of commerce, Mali's rulers maintained the grandeur of their empire.

important to Muslims, who also excelled in the arts of medicine, astronomy, mathematics, and geography. Having lived simply in farming and fishing communities, with highly developed oral traditions and religious rituals, West Africans had not felt the need for the literary arts. However, as the West Africans of the cities adopted Islam in greater numbers, they increasingly acquired the skills of reading and writing. As Djibril Niane has indicated, "As a patron and friend of literature, Musa helped lay the foundation of the Arabic literature of the blacks which was to bear its first fruit in the cities of Jenne and Timbuktu in the fourteenth and sixteenth centuries."

The Muslim law courts were also quite distinctive, as they applied the teachings of the Koran to every aspect of life. Muslim judges, called *qadis*, possessed wide-ranging powers to inflict punishment, including the death penalty, on offenders. Islamic law differed considerably from the customary laws of the Sudanese, which were not written down but rather passed on from one generation to the next. Whereas Islamic law stressed individual responsibility for misdeeds, African law made the family or the clan, or both, accountable for any crimes committed by individual mem-

bers. Like many other peoples living in traditional societies, West Africans relied more on the principles of conciliation and compensation than physical punishment. The practice of cutting off the hands of a thief, common in Muslim nations, was unacceptable to West Africans, who expected the culprit's family to make good for the theft. Even a case of murder could be resolved by a gift of cattle or other goods to the relatives of the victim. In cases cited by John S. Trimingham in his book *Islam in West Africa*, the compensation for murder was set at 100 oxen, 50 to be paid by the chief of the clan and 50 by the murderer's family.

Dire punishments were not unheard-of among the Sudanese, however. A murder victim's family was free to reject compensation and seek blood revenge; people convicted of harming others through sorcery could be put to death; and those who offended the king often forfeited their lives. But as was the case with West African religion, maintaining the proper balance of things was more important than following the strict rules of punishment specified by Islamic law. For this reason, West Africans who converted to Islam often chose to avoid the judgment of the qadi. They went instead to another official known as the *khatib*

35

(preacher) who was more likely to settle a case through conciliation—even, at times, applying the customary law instead of Islamic law.

Ibn Battuta, a distinguished Muslim scholar who visited Mali during the reign of Mansa Musa's successor, Mansa Suleyman (1337–60), was deeply impressed by the moral character of the Sudanese: "They are seldom unjust, and have a greater abhorrence of injustice than any other people. . . . There is complete security in their country. Neither traveller nor inhabitant in it has anything to fear from robbers or men of violence. They do not confiscate the property of any white man who dies in their country, even if it be uncounted wealth. On the contrary, they give it into the charge of some trustworthy person among the whites, until the rightful heir takes possession of it."

At first, Ibn Battuta was less impressed by the generosity of Mansa Suleyman, whom he compared unfavorably to Mansa Musa. (Mansa Musa, he pointed out with approval, once gave the architect as-Sahili 4,000 dinars in a single day.) After spending four months in Mali without receiving any sort of gift, he was bold enough to voice a complaint at the king's audience. Mansa Suleyman had apparently not been informed that Ibn Battuta was in Mali; the king immediately provided a house for the distinguished visitor and gave him a sum of money for expenses. Thus appeased, Ibn Battuta admitted that the royal court made a splendid spectacle:

> On certain days the sultan holds audiences in the palace yard, where there is a platform under a tree, with three steps; this they call the *pempi*. It is carpeted with silk and has cushions placed on it. [Over it] is raised the umbrella, which is a sort of pavilion made of silk, surmounted by a bird in gold, about the size of a falcon. The sultan comes out of a door in a corner of the palace, carrying a bow in his hand and a quiver on his back. On his head he has a golden skull-cap, bound with a gold band which has narrow ends shaped like knives, more than a span in length. His usual dress is a velvety red tunic, made of the European fabrics called *mutanfas*. The sultan is preceded by his musicians, who carry gold and silver guimbris [two-stringed guitars], and behind him come three hundred armed slaves. . . . On reaching the *pempi* he stops and looks around the assembly, then ascends it in the sedate manner of a preacher ascending a mosque-pulpit. As he takes his seat the drums, trumpets, and bugles are sounded.

تمبوكتو ٥٢ يوما
TOMBOUCTOU 52 JOURS

A directional sign in present-day Morocco points the way to Timbuktu, an estimated 52-day journey across the Sahara Desert. As in the days of ancient Mali, the camel remains the principal means of crossing the Sahara.

Ultimately, the splendor of the royal court derived from Mali's position at the hub of West Africa's most important trade routes, along which great caravans made their way into the empire from the east and the north. During Mali's greatest days, the most important route began at Sijilmasa in North Africa, and it was this route that Ibn Battuta took to reach Niani. At Sijilmasa, North African merchants collected goods such as silks, glassware, and copper and loaded their wares onto camels for the journey across the desert. The first important stop for the caravans, after more than 20 days of traveling, was Teghaza, the site of the great Saharan salt mines. At Teghaza, salt was dug from the earth like stone and cut into blocks that were each three feet long and a foot wide. Salt was the essential item in the trade for Sudanese gold because it was generally lacking in the vegetarian diet of the Sudanese. In hot climates, where the body rapidly loses essential minerals through perspiration, both humans and animals become quickly exhausted without an adequate daily salt intake. For this reason, the peoples of the interior were willing to trade their gold for a substance that is now a common household item: as Ibn Battuta points out, a load of salt sold for 8 to 10 dinars in the Sahara, whereas in Mali it would fetch 20 to 30 dinars, and sometimes as much as 40. Among themselves, West Africans were known to use small chunks of salt in place of money.

From Teghaza, the caravans traveled another 10 days until they reached Tasarahla, where there were underground supplies of water. Then the most

A group of traders, their camels bearing slabs of salt, assemble in a square in Timbuktu. In order to survive the arduous trek across the Sahara, North African merchants had to carefully plan every aspect of their journey.

difficult and dangerous part of the journey began. "From this point the *takshif* is despatched," Ibn Battuta recounted. "The *takshif* . . . is hired by the persons in the caravan to go ahead to Iwálátan [Walata], carrying letters from them to their friends there. . . . These persons then come out a distance of four nights' journey to meet the caravan, and bring water with them. . . . It often happens that the *takshif* perishes in this desert, with the result that the people of Iwálátan know nothing about the caravan, and all or most of those who are with it perish."

Those merchants who were fortunate enough to reach Walata could then transport their goods more easily to Timbuktu, Jenne, Gao, and the other cities of Mali. The entire journey from Sijilmasa to the center of Mali took about two months. In order to provide order and safety for the passage of these caravans, the mansas of Mali had achieved feats of political organization that placed them on a level with any rulers in the world.

Chapter 5 | THE GRANDEUR OF EMPIRE

A 14th century terra-cotta horse and rider from Jenne, Mali, measuring 66 X 38 X 12 cm. According to historians, Mali's elite cavalry was the backbone of a highly disciplined 100,000-man army.

At its height, the empire of Mali encompassed a territory that extended from Tadmekka in the east all the way to the Atlantic coast, a distance of about 700 miles. The total population of the empire is estimated to have been 40–50 million. The administration of such an empire was a tremendous challenge, owing especially to the difficulty of linking the outlying districts with the capital. The majority of people did not read or write, and all communications had to be transmitted verbally by messengers who traveled from place to place on horseback. Clearly, the mansas could not govern their vast territory from Niani on a day-to-day basis without a sophisticated political organization.

After his victory at Kirina in 1240, Sundiata met with the Mandingo chiefs at Kangaba. There, the victorious leaders organized Mali into a number of provinces. Those regions that had rallied to Sundiata during his struggle with Sumanguru were allowed a large degree of independence under their traditional rulers. On the other hand, the provinces that Sundiata had been forced to subdue were to be governed by an official known as a *farin*, who transmitted Sundiata's wishes to the chiefs of the Malinke villages. The dignitaries of Sundiata's court in Niani were chosen from his closest supporters and his military commanders, and the followers of various crafts and professions were organized into he-

The Kamablon, an ancient Mandingo shrine in the town of Ka-ba (formerly Kangaba), Mali. At Kangaba, the victorious Sundiata met with his commanders and organized the government of his kingdom. Every seven years, the Mandingo gather at the Kamablon to celebrate this event.

42

reditary groups. The sons of fishermen, weavers, or blacksmiths were expected to take up their fathers' trades.

By the time of Mansa Musa and Mansa Suleyman, the empire of Mali consisted of 12 provinces, among them the formerly independent states of Ghana and Takrur. The provinces apparently had a great deal of independence, but the mansas exerted strict control over many aspects of Mali's life, such as trade, finance, and food production. In order to oversee these functions, the mansas relied upon a number of high officials in the royal court.

Perhaps the most important of these was the griot, the mansa's spokesman, who was chosen from the Kouyate clan, to which Sundiata's first griot, Balla Fasseke, had belonged. In order to emphasize his authority, the mansa never spoke directly to any of his subjects. He spoke in a low voice to the griot, and the griot loudly repeated his words. Needless to say, anyone who wished to approach the emperor had to do so through the griot. According to Djibiril Niane, the griot also had other important functions: "Couriers left Niani daily on horseback, and those who arrived from the provinces reported to the *griot.* He was the tutor of princes; it was he who conducted ceremonies and directed the court musicians."

In addition to the griot, the mansa had a circle of advisers who corresponded to the cabinet ministers of modern governments. The *khalissi-farma* looked after the empire's finances; relations with foreigners were handled by the *korei-farma;* agriculture was the responsibility of the *babili-farma;* the *tu-tigui* managed the forests; the *dji-tigui* managed the fisheries in the Niger River; and the inspector general of the entire empire was known as the *kanfari.* By adopting this sophisticated level of organization, the kings of Mali went beyond the achievements of ancient Ghana and began a new chapter in West African history.

Mali's army, which was most likely about 100,000 strong, was also carefully organized and equipped. As Djibril Niane

43

A Bambara wood carving of a seated figure holding a lance. During the 17th century, the Bambara kingdoms of Segu and Kaarta rose to prominence in West Africa.

has written, "The strength of the army lay in the warlike nature and sense of discipline of the Mandingo, who were the army's most important element. . . . The aristocracy or 'nobility of the quiver' [descended from the comrades of Sundiata] were soldiers by choice. The cavalry was made up of *ton-tigui* or quiver-bearers; from Sundiata's time, it was an élite corps. . . . A Mandingo cavalryman would be armed with long spears and sabres in addition to his bow and arrows. As an élite corps, the cavalry was directly under the orders of the mansa. The infantry was commanded by the minor nobility. They were armed with lances or quivers according to the area from which they came: Mande soldiers usually had bows and arrows; those from the Sahara usually carried skin shields and fought with lances."

With these powerful forces garrisoned in such outposts as Walata, Gao, Timbuktu, and Niani, the mansas were able to provide security for the traders and their caravans. As the widely traveled Ibn Battuta noted with approval, Mansa Musa and his successors had created a state of "complete and general safety" within the huge territory of Mali. Equally important, the ministers in charge of regulating food production had suc-

ceeded in creating a land of plenty: cattle, sheep, goats, and chickens were raised throughout Mali, and farmers grew a variety of crops, such as rice, millet, beans, and yams. The fishing clans hauled in their catches up and down the Niger, so that dried and smoked fish could be had even in areas far from the river. According to Ibn Battuta, food was so abundant and inexpensive that travelers did not have to worry about carrying supplies— they could find whatever they needed in each city or village that they visited.

It should not be supposed, however, that commerce and war were the only talents of Mali's people. Though the Arab writers were more interested in the social and political features of the Sudan, archaeologists exploring the region near Jenne during the 1970s found numerous small sculptures of exceptional beauty. Crafted in terra-cotta, a variety of clay that becomes extremely hard when baked, the figures were made between A.D. 1000 and 1400. Many represent human forms, often in kneeling postures, and are thought to represent the ancestors of those for whom the sculptures were made. Others portray figures on horseback, perhaps glorifying the monarchy and the military prowess of Mali. Still others are of animals, such as monkeys,

(Continued on page 49)

44

ART OF THE DOGON AND BAMBARA

The artwork on these pages was created for use in religious rites of the Dogon and Bambara peoples of Mali. The Dogon have a highly complex religion that is little understood by Western anthropologists.

A wooden stool used by the hogan, *the Dogon spiritual leader. The eight sculpted figures represent the Nommo, the mythical ancestors of the Dogon.*

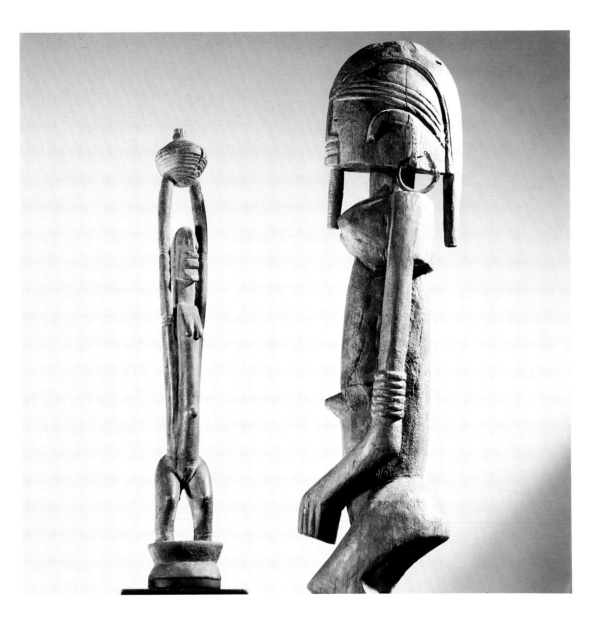

Two sculptures, made of wood, metal, and beads, that were kept in the house of the hogan and used during burial ceremonies.

Wrought iron equestrian figure that may represent the mythical blacksmith who brought the ancestors to earth and gave them skills and crafts.

Wooden Bambara dance mask.

(Continued from page 44)

lizards, dogs, birds, fish, and snakes, the latter having wide religious significance in West Africa. In his *Short History of African Art,* Werner Gillon writes, "The kneeling figures have been stylized in an astonishing way. The body leans back slightly, the thighs and legs forming the base, with the legs often indicated only by a dividing line. . . . There are a few sculptures of couples with the hands of the seated male placed protectively on the shoulders of the female kneeling in front of him. In the faces of many figures, seated and kneeling, the artists were able to express strong emotions—fear, compassion, anguish, serenity, and tenderness."

Compared with the prosperous and peaceful society that produced such works, the state of Europe in the 14th century was hardly impressive. During that period, the life of Europe was dominated by the Hundred Years War, a series of bloody conflicts between France and England arising from England's claim to various French territories. The war, which raged on and off between 1337 and 1453, left much of France in ruins. In addition, all of Europe was devastated by the Black Death, an outbreak of bubonic plague that wiped out one-third of the total population by 1350. The economies of nations collapsed; peasant revolts broke out in France and England; religious life was disrupted by a lack of clergy and the rise of fanatical sects; learning and culture declined with the death of Europe's leading scholars. Nothing could have been further removed from the bustling cities of Mali, with their mosques and neat brick houses and their markets filled with goods.

49

Chapter 6 | THE END OF EMPIRE

This Dogon village has been erected in the shelter of the Bandiagara cliffs in the Republic of Mali. The fiercely independent Dogon, noted for their sophisticated religious ideas and remarkable artwork, were never subdued by the ancient kings of Mali; they have maintained their unique way of life to the present day.

At their height, empires appear destined to last forever, but even the greatest have failed to endure for more than a century or two. In the case of Mali, imperial power depended to a large extent on the personal qualities of leaders such as Sundiata, Mansa Musa, and Mansa Suleyman. After the death of Suleyman in 1360, the royal palace in Niani was occupied by a series of second-rate rulers who were increasingly unable to command loyalty or obedience. The mansas and the local chiefs continued to practice Islam, but the people of the countryside—and in some cases entire Mandingo states, such as Kaabu in the west—clung fiercely to their ancestral religions. Thus, while Islam had forged powerful links between Mali and the rest of the world, it had also created tensions that rebellious local chiefs could turn to their advantage.

The restiveness and ambition of neighboring peoples posed an even greater challenge to the rulers of Mali. By 1400, the rich city of Gao on the Niger had declared its independence and was no longer paying taxes to the mansas. (Before long, Gao was to form one of the centers of Songhay, a new and even greater empire.) At the same time, the Tuareg of the southern Sahara Desert swept into Mali's northernmost territories, capturing the important trading cities of Walata and Timbuktu during the 1430s. In the west, the Fulani embarked on a series of wars against the kings of Mali during the late 15th and early 16th centuries, pressing steadily southward toward the Casamance and Gambia riv-

52

ers. As Madina Ly-Tall, a historian at the present-day University of Mali, has written, "In the late fifteenth and early sixteenth centuries . . . we have a narrowing of the corridor linking eastern and western Mali. Mandingo traders sent by the Mali mansa to sell gold at the Sutuco market in Gambia were no longer safe. They had to make many detours, so that their journey sometimes took more than six months."

The final blow to Mali's power in the Sudan occurred at the very end of the 16th century, in 1599. At that time, Mansa Mahmud IV attempted to capture the city of Jenne, which had been part of the empire of Songhay but had recently been captured by an invading force from Morocco. However, Mahmud was betrayed by one of the Fulani chiefs who had previously agreed to join him, and the Moroccans were able to win the battle. The mansas were still held in such esteem that the Fulani chiefs rode after Mahmud as he fled the battle, seeking to ensure his safety and to pay their personal respects to him. But the real power of Mali was gone. By the 17th century, the territory of Mali was hardly larger than it had been before the rise of Sundiata.

The cultural and economic influence of Mali, on the other hand, was never extinguished. During the great days of the empire, a new class of Muslim traders known as the Wangara had developed among the Mandingo. They began to establish trade routes throughout West Africa as early as the 14th century, spreading Islam as they sold their goods. As the empire of Mali declined, more and more of the Wangara migrated to the forest belt in the south, bordering the Gulf of Guinea. In this region, they developed a trade in kola nuts, grown only in the forest regions, and assisted in exploiting the wealth of new goldfields. When merchants from the European nation of Portugal reached the Atlantic coast of Africa during the 15th century, they were deeply impressed with the trading skill of the Wangara, who remain a vital force in the economy of present-day West Africa.

During the 16th and 17th centuries, the kingdom of Kaabu emerged as the most powerful state in Mali's former territory, but the peace and prosperity that had marked the reign of the mansas was long gone. The French, English, and Dutch followed the Portuguese in penetrating the interior of Africa, and before long the transatlantic slave trade was disrupting the societies of the Sudan. African kings made war upon their neighbors in order to capture prisoners who were then sold to the slave traders; in this way, many of West Africa's healthiest men and women were shipped off to an uncertain fate in the Americas. Even under these adverse conditions, the culture of Mali remained vital: the Dogon and

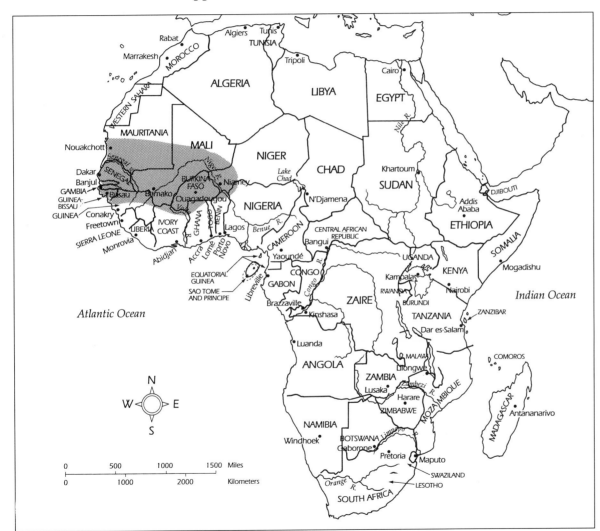

53

A map of contemporary Africa; the territory formerly controlled by the empire of Mali now lies mainly within the nations of Mali, Mauritania, Senegal, and Burkina Faso.

Tellem peoples continued the brilliant artistic tradition begun in the region of Jenne during the great days of the empire. As late as the 18th century, when Mungo Park visited the former Malian city of Segu, he found it thriving under the Bambara ruler Mansoun.

When the European powers finally carved up Africa late in the 19th century, most of Mali's former territory came under the control of the French. However, the French did not find it easy to subdue the proud West Africans. The opposition to colonial rule was led by Somori Ture, a Mandingo ruler who commanded a well-equipped army of some 40,000 men. (The army's modern weapons were paid for in part with the proceeds from the Bure goldfields, which were still producing mineral wealth.) Beginning in 1885, Somori waged a series of successful campaigns against the French invaders, inflicting heavy losses on them and keeping them at bay for nearly 15 years. Only after capturing Somori during a surprise attack in 1898 were the French able to gain control of the Mandingo lands.

During the colonial period, Mali's former territory became known as the French Sudan. After the end of World War II in 1945, the peoples of Africa began an irrepressible movement for independence, and on September 22, 1960, the Republic of Mali was born, with its capital located at Bamako on the Niger. The nation's first president was Modibo Keita, a leader in the fight for independence and a member of the same clan as the great lord Sundiata.

Today, the nation of Mali encompasses many of the peoples who created West Africa's great empires: the Soninke, the Songhay, the Fulani, the Bambara, and the Malinke. The nation also numbers among its citizens the Tuareg of the southern Sahara, who continue to live as wandering herders. Thus Mali remains an important crossroads for African cultures. As in the days of empire, Islam remains Mali's official religion, and the Mande language predominates. Among Malians, the empire created by Sundiata and his successors remains a living presence. In many villages, the griots still relate the chronicles of Mali's great kings. This is especially true in Kangaba, the age-old center of Malinke culture; there, the Malinke gather every seven years to reenact the building of a sanctuary known as the Kamablon and to celebrate the events that made Mali one of the world's great empires.

Mali today depends on agriculture, with almost 75 percent of the population

A modern-day Malian griot plays the kora, a traditional West African instrument. The griots of Mali and Senegal continue to recite the great events of their peoples' history; scholars have drawn on their accounts in order to understand the African past.

engaged in food production. During the 1980s, Malians suffered greatly from the prolonged drought that afflicted the western Sudan. In response, the government of Mali began the Senegal River Valley Development, an ambitious project designed to harness the waters of the river for electrical power, irrigation, and the development of fisheries. As their country strives to meet new challenges, Malians draw inspiration from their brilliant legacy. As the griot Mamadou Kouyate sings to all who wish to learn, "Mali is eternal."

CHRONOLOGY

10th–11th centuries	Ancient Ghana reaches the height of its power
12th century	Ghana's empire dissolves as focus of gold trade shifts to the territory of the Malinke
1203	Sumanguru Kante, king of the Soso, conquers the Malinke and controls the Niger River region
1240	Sundiata Keita defeats Sumanguru at the Battle of Kirina; Sundiata transforms Mali into a unified state
1241–70	Reign of Sundiata as king of Mali; Mali develops the most sophisticated political organization yet seen in West Africa
1312	Mansa Musa begins reign as king of Mali; during his rule, Mali reaches the height of its power and fame
1324–26	Mansa Musa makes pilgrimage to Mecca; Islamic influences become evident in Mali's architecture, society, and culture
1337	Death of Mansa Musa
1337–1453	Hundred Years War rages in Europe, devastating much of France
1337–60	Reign of Mansa Suleyman, the last great king of Mali

1347–50	One-third of Europe's population is wiped out by the bubonic plague, or Black Death
1352	Ibn Battuta visits Mali
1430s	Tuareg raiders capture trading centers of Walata and Timbuktu; power and wealth of Mali begin to decline
1599	Mansa Mahmud IV is defeated by Moroccans at Jenne; decline of Mali is complete
1960	Mali is reborn as a modern republic on September 22

FURTHER READING

Bloch, Marc. *Feudal Society.* Translated by L. A. Manyon. Chicago: University of Chicago Press, 1961.

Connah, Graham. *African Civilizations.* Cambridge: Cambridge University Press, 1987.

Davidson, Basil. *Africa in History.* Rev. ed. New York: Collier, 1991.

———. *The African Genius.* Boston: Little, Brown, 1969.

———. *The Lost Cities of Africa.* Rev. ed. Boston: Little, Brown, 1987.

Davidson, Basil, with F. K. Buah and the advice of J. F. A. Ajayi. *A History of West Africa, 1000–1800.* Rev. ed. London: Longman, 1977.

Garlake, Peter. *The Kingdoms of Africa.* New York: Bedrick, 1990.

Gillon, Werner. *A Short History of African Art.* New York: Penguin, 1986.

Hull, Richard W. *African Cities and Towns Before the European Conquest.* New York: Norton, 1976.

Ibn Battuta. *Travels in Asia and Africa.* Translated by H. A. R. Gibb. London: Routledge, 1957.

Koslow, Philip. *Centuries of Greatness: The West African Kingdoms, 750–1900.* New York: Chelsea House, 1994.

Kwamwena-Poh, Michael, et al. *African History in Maps.* London: Longman, 1982.

Levtzion, Nehemiah. *Ancient Ghana and Mali.* New York: Africana, 1980.

Levtzion, Nehemiah, and J. F. G. Hopkins. *Corpus of Early Arabic Sources for West African History.* Cambridge: Cambridge University Press, 1981.

Naylor, Kim. *Mali.* New York: Chelsea House, 1987.

Niane, Djibril. *Sundiata: An Epic of Old Mali.* Translated by G. D. Pickett. London: Longman, 1965.

Oliver, Roland, and Anthony Atmore. *Africa Since 1800.* 3rd ed. Cambridge: Cambridge University Press, 1981.

Oliver, Roland, and B. M. Fagan. *Africa in the Iron Age.* Cambridge: Cambridge University Press, 1975.

Previté-Orton, C. W. *The Shorter Cambridge Medieval History.* 2 vols. Cambridge: Cambridge University Press, 1952.

Trimingham, John S. *Islam in West Africa.* London: University of Oxford Press, 1962.

UNESCO General History of Africa. 7 vols. Berkeley: University of California Press 1980-92.

GLOSSARY

archaeology   the study of the physical remains of past human societies

clan   a social group united by descent from a common ancestor; also known as a descent line

conversion   the act of renouncing one religion and adopting another

dinar   basic gold coin of the Muslim world, equal to one *mitqal*

griot   (gree-OH) an important official in the royal court of Mali; in modern times, an African storyteller who preserves the oral traditions of a people; also known by the title of *djeli*

Islam   the world religion that is based upon worship of Allah and acceptance of Muhammad as his prophet

kafu   a traditional community of the Mandingo consisting of a group of villages with a total population of 10,000 to 50,000

Kamablon   a sanctuary in the village of Kangaba, Mali, where the Malinke hold an important ritual every seven years

khatib   a Muslim preacher who also functions as a judge

Mandingo   Mande-speaking people who include the Malinke and Bambara; also known as Mandinka and Mande

mansa   Mande word meaning "lord"; title adopted by the kings of Mali

mitqal	basic monetary unit of the Muslim world, equal to one-eighth of an ounce of gold; known as a dinar when in the form of gold coinage
Muslim	one who follows the religion of Islam
oral tradition	a form of historical record in which events are passed on through generations of storytellers instead of being written down
pempi	a ceremonial platform on which the kings of Mali sat when receiving their subjects
pilgrimage	a journey to a shrine or holy place
qadi	a Muslim judge possessing wide powers to settle civil and criminal cases
Soninke	Mande-speaking West Africans who founded the states of Wagadu and ancient Ghana
Sudan	the region of sub-Saharan Africa stretching from the Atlantic coast to the valley of the Nile River
Wangara	Mandingo people who converted to Islam and became powerful traders; also known as the Dyula

INDEX

63

PHILIP KOSLOW earned his B.A. and M.A. degrees from New York University and went on to teach and conduct research at Oxford University, where his interest in medieval European and African history was awakened. The editor of numerous volumes for young adults, he is also the author of *Centuries of Greatness: The West African Kingdoms, 750–1900* in the Chelsea House series MILESTONES IN BLACK AMERICAN HISTORY and of *Ancient Ghana: The Land of Gold*, the first volume of THE KINGDOMS OF AFRICA.

PICTURE CREDITS